Endangered Animals

Wildlife around the World People Must Protect

Written by Jo A. Steele
Illustrated by Richard Eijkenbroek

◆ FriesenPress

Suite 300 - 990 Fort St
Victoria, BC, V8V 3K2
Canada

www.friesenpress.com

Copyright © 2017 by Jo A. Steele
First Edition — 2017

All rights reserved.

No part of this publication may be reproduced in any form, or by any means, electronic or mechanical, including photocopying, recording, or any information browsing, storage, or retrieval system, without permission in writing from FriesenPress.

ISBN
978-1-4602-9413-0 (Paperback)
978-1-4602-9414-7 (eBook)

1. JUVENILE NONFICTION, ANIMALS, ENDANGERED

Distributed to the trade by The Ingram Book Company

To
my grandparents,
Herbert E. Hamly (1903–1985)
Dorothy C. Hamly (1904–2001)
for teaching me to appreciate wildlife,

and to,
my family,
for caring for all animals

Introduction

Would you like to keep enjoying and smelling flowers, observing and marveling at wildlife, and travelling to beautiful, exotic environments? Then you should know about the International Union for Conservation of Nature (IUCN), a worldwide alliance dedicated to the protection and preservation of threatened species and habitats in which they are trying to thrive. In addition, the Canadian Wildlife Federation (CWF) works toward saving endangered species and their environments in Canada, and I would like to donate 5% of each Endangered Animals book sold to the CWF, a most worthy organization that I am happy to promote. I would also like to further the education of children with regard to animals that are in need of our attention lest they vanish from Earth. To that end, there is a glossary at end of the book. Finally, the information reported in these pages was found during 2014-2016, but keep in mind ... sadly the list of endangered wildlife continues to grow.

ELEPHANTS love to keep cool by rolling in the mud, sucking water into their trunks, and spraying themselves. They store the water in pouches deep in their throat, and when temperatures rise, they're ready to beat the heat!

BIGHORN SHEEP climb high in the mountains and come down to find water to drink and greenery to eat. The males, called rams, are well known for their strong, round horns. The females, called ewes, also have horns, but they are smaller and not as curved.

CROCODILES have short, strong legs with sharp claws to help them fight and capture their prey. They have eyes, ears, and nostrils set on top of their heads, which allows them to keep breathing, even if the rest of their bodies are submerged in the water.

CHIMPANZEES form their nests on the tops of trees using tree branches and leafage. They sleep in these nests, safe from invaders. Strangely, however, they will smile when they are frightened.

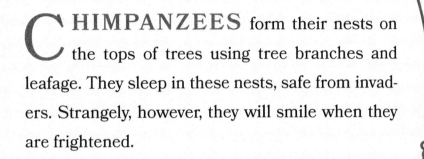

L IONS can see five times better than humans, which helps them to be great hunters. Interestingly enough, even though a male lion is known as the "King of the Jungle," a female lion, called a lioness, is actually the better hunter of the two.

B LUE WHALES are the biggest animals alive. Their hearts may be as big as a small car and their tongues as heavy as an adult elephant. They are extremely loud and can hear each other's songs from distances as far as Edmonton, in Alberta, Canada to Casper, Wyoming in the United States.

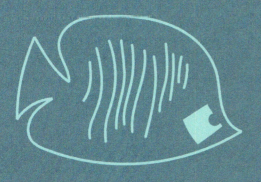

GRAY WOLVES live and hunt together in a pack. Their leaders, called the alpha male and female, eat first after the prey is caught. Their teeth are razor sharp for hunting, killing, and eating their catch. Wolves also howl to mark their area, talk to their pack, and say "Hello" to another pack.

POLAR BEARS love to play in the snow, and can swim as much as 48 kilometers or 30 miles. Their unique paws with dots, called papillae, are specialized to keep them from sliding on ice and to make it easier to catch fish when bigger prey, like seals, are not available.

INDIANA BATS, which grow only up to two inches, gather by the thousands in limestone caves to spend their winter. Sleeping during the cold months and awakening in the warm spring, when there are plenty of insects for them to eat, is called hibernation.

SIBERIAN TIGERS are the biggest cats in the world, with full manes to keep them warm in the mountains. The adult male can weigh more than 320 kilograms or 700 pounds, which is the size of a large piano, while the female weighs a little more than half that much.

CRIMSON WING FLAMINGOS are born white or gray, but when they mature, their feathers are bright pink or cherry red. The dazzling color of adult flamingos comes from the algae and aquatic life they eat, which is loaded with carotene, a coloring substance that makes carrots orange.

KOALAS are not actually bears. In fact, they are related to kangaroos and wombats! Their long pointed claws, strong legs, and curved backbones help them when climbing and resting in eucalyptus trees.

SEA OTTERS have long flexible bodies for easy swimming. They have two layers of thick fur to keep them warm in cold water and they can weigh up to 45 kilograms or 100 pounds, which is about as much as a large television!

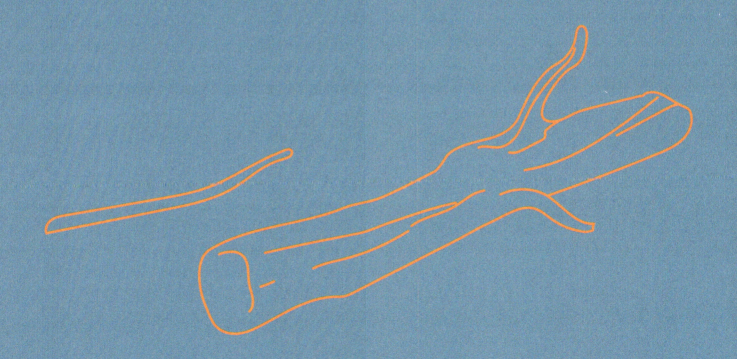

BLACK RHINOCEROSES have two horns in front to fight invaders and protect their family. Rhinos, as they are commonly called, have excellent senses of smell and hearing, but their sight is weak, which can cause them to be more uncertain when danger is present.

GREEN SEA TURTLES are the largest hard shell reptiles in the sea turtle family. They are cold-blooded, making it easier to hold their breath for hours when in icy waters. They are known to have a lifespan of up to 80 years!

EMPEROR PENGUINS are the biggest of their species, weighing from 27 to 41 kilograms or 60 to 90 pounds. They live on the open ice areas in the Antarctic, gathering close together to help avoid the wind, and to maintain their body heat.

RED EYED TREE FROGS have bright red eyes, yellowish-orange webbed feet, and long sticky tongues to help them hunt through the night. They have suction tapes on their feet, which make them ideal climbers and jumpers!

Glossary

AQUATIC	living or growing in water
CAROTENE	yellow or orange pigments found in plants, which are transformed into vitamin A in the liver
CONSERVATION	protection and restoration of nature
ENDANGERED	threatened with extinction
EXTINCTION	dying out and no longer existing
FAUNA	Latin word for animals of a certain area
SPECIES	a class of living beings that share common characteristics
THREATENED	likely to become endangered
WILDLIFE	animals living in the uncivilized areas

Webpages

www.animalfactguide.com/animal-facts

www.animalstime.com/endangered-animals-for-kids

www.buzzle.com

www.ehow.com/facts_5179103_endangered-animals-information-kids.html

www.kids.nationalgeographic.com

www.kidsplanet.org

Jo A. Steele

Jo A. Steele was born in Edmonton, Alberta in 1964, and she holds a Bachelor of Arts in Applied Psychology. Today she lives approximately 116 kilometers northeast of her birthplace in the Canadian town of Smoky Lake, also known as the Pumpkin Capital of Alberta. She is a nurse's aide and a childcare worker. It is Ms. Steele's love of children and animals, as well as her interest in helping endangered wildlife that drew her to write this book.

CPSIA information can be obtained
at www.ICGtesting.com
Printed in the USA
LVOW05s1520300717
543035LV00010BC/10/P